Complaint in the Garden

Winner of the 2003

Kenyon Review Prize in Poetry

Complaint in the Garden

Randall Mann

Zoo Press

Copyright © 2004 by Randall Mann • All rights reserved

Zoo Press • P.O. Box 22990 • Lincoln, Nebraska • 68542
Printed in the United States of America

Sponsored by *The Kenyon Review*
104 College Drive • Gambier, Ohio • 43022-2693

Cover art © Debora Greger, "At the Edge of the Garden, where the Grounds
of Memory Start," 1993, paper sewn to paper with metallic thread

Cover design by Janice Clark of Good Studio © 2003
www.goodstudio.com

Distributed to the trade by The University of Nebraska Press
Lincoln, Nebraska • 68588 • www.nebraskapress.unl.edu

Library of Congress Cataloging-in-Publication Data

Mann, Randall.
  Complaint in the garden : poems / by Randall Mann.-- 1st ed.
    p. cm.
  ISBN 1-932023-12-7 (alk. paper)
  I. Title.
PS3613.A55 C66 2004
811'.6--dc22
                                        2003022092

zoo022

Acknowledgments

Grateful acknowledgment is made to the editors of the following publications, where these poems, often in slightly different form, first appeared:

32 Poems: "Complaint, Poolside"; *America:* "Yard Sale"; *American Literary Review:* "The New World"; *Antioch Review:* "Translation of the Confessionario* into the Local Dialect"; *Chelsea:* "?" and "The Landscape of Deception"; *Christian Science Monitor:* "Angel in Florida" (under the title "Dust and Broughtonia") and "Out on the Porch"; *Formalist:* "Henry James in Jacksonville" and "Je n'ai pas oublié"; *Gay & Lesbian Review:* "Late Epithalamion"; *Gulf Coast:* "The Shortened History of Florida"; *Kenyon Review:* "Complaint in the Garden," "The Lady Wishfort," "Rain," and "Social Life"; *Lodestar Quarterly:* "Old Haunts" and "The Future Tense"; *National Poetry Review:* "Lament"; *New Republic:* "The Mote in the Eye" (part I of "The Elements"); *Paris Review:* "Evidence" and "Poem Beginning with a Line by John Ashbery"; *Poetry:* "Fiduciary"; *Prairie Schooner:* "Blood," "The End of the Last Summer," and "Song"; *Quarterly West:* "Postscriptum"; *Salmagundi:* "The Beauty of Things," "Complaint of the Lecturer," "The Manmade Lake" (part III of "The Elements"), and "South"; *Seneca Review:* "The Heron" and "Pantoum"; *Sewanee Theological Review:* "The English Angler" (under the title "The English Angler in Florida") and "The Revival of Vernacular Architecture" (part II of "The Elements"); *Western Humanities Review:* "Complaint of the Regular" and "Eros."

"Angel in Florida" (under the title "Dust and Broughtonia") appeared in *American Diaspora: Poetry of Displacement*, Virgil Suárez and Ryan G. Van Cleave, eds. (University of Iowa Press, 2001).

"Fiduciary" appeared in *Writing Poems*, Robert Wallace and Michelle Boisseau, eds. (Longman, 2004).

"Fiduciary" also appeared in *Poetry Daily: 366 Poems from the World's Most Popular Poetry Website*, Don Selby, Diane Boller, and Chryss Yost, eds. (Sourcebooks, 2003).

"Elegy for the Hurdler" appeared in *Bend, Don't Shatter*, T. Cole Rachel and Rita D. Costello, eds. (Soft Skull Press, 2004).

"The New World" and "Fiduciary" appeared as the poems of the day for January 15, 2001, and July 8, 2002, respectively, at the *Poetry Daily* website (http://www.poems.com).

Thank you to those who read these poems in drafts—in particular, my teachers.

For a Tennessee Williams Scholarship in 1996, I would like to thank the Sewanee Writers' Conference.

Thanks to my mother, father, and sister for their love and support.

for George O. Kolombatovich

Table of Contents

On Mann's *Complaint in the Garden*

Following Beth Ann Fennelly's *Open House* (2001) and Christopher Cessac's *Republic Sublime* (2002), Randall Mann takes his place in 2003 as the winner of the Kenyon Review Prize in Poetry. From among the hundreds of manuscripts submitted, Mann's *Complaint in the Garden* quickly asserted itself for its rich idiom, its technical command, its poignant, often overlapping narratives, and its coherence not just as a miscellany but as a real book of poems. This last feature is not a necessity, to my mind, as I read a poet's collection. But in Mann's case, some of the considerable power of the poetry derived from the moving, well-wrought wholeness of the book itself, with its sense of progression, its dramatic yet controlled directions.

The largest or most historically sizable narrative in *Complaint in the Garden* stems from Mann's Southern background. I admire his natural-historian's gifts, to observe and record with care. He recreates the landscape and flora of the Caribbean and Florida with great precision, its saw palmettos and egrets, its "feathery-leafed locusts" and "punctual monsoons." He follows, in other words, a long line of observers from Donald Justice back through William Bartram to Ponce de León and Cabeza de Vaca. Like Justice—a clear poetic influence—he renders the lush American tropics in sensuous but spare formal language, establishing a languid, rain-logged, fertile milieu. And like the earlier explorers, he is avid to investigate the garden-world before him, where he finds not just "water lilies slowly moving toward the shore" but also "gold, like lightning" and "long-robed friars" among the "pockmarked bellboys." Part of Mann's project is to

trace the collision of natural and human cultures that has character-
ized his beloved Southeast, and this continent, for the past five hundred years.

But let me show you what I mean. Mann's style is so finely
tuned throughout the thirty-seven poems of *Complaint in the
Garden*, his touch so various—delicate, playful, brooding—that I'd
like to include here a whole poem to represent the subtle capabilties
of his art. This is, simply enough, "The Heron":

A pond the color of Oriental teas.
A heron refusing to look anywhere but east.

Mangroves flecked with a fire,
deep-set birches rife

with the wait for night. In stone,
the heron stares: the stoic tones

of the sky a storied procession of palms;
their red-tipped fronds, overhanging lamps.

Water-bird, it has been centuries since I felt
anything for you. You have been left:

look around. Why does the owl
rest on a goddess's shoulder while you wade so low?

Deep within the Southern landscape, perched just above the surface of a pond at evening, the heron seems both at home and easy to

miss. Or is the heron a statue, a remnant "in stone" of a time when gods and goddesses endowed birds with supernatural power? Mann's imagery—precise, select, graceful—is akin to early Chinese lyrics. Even the heron gazes nowhere "but east." Mann has absorbed the wonderful paradox so central to Chinese lyrics: To suggest silence and stillness in a poem, the details must provide a touch of sound, a hint of movement. I find further delight in the posture or configuration of the poem. The bird, the trees, the burning sky, all overlook the still water, and the reflection of each thing is cast back upward, with a slight wrinkle. That's the function of the couplet here, with one body, one line, set atop another; and that's the function of the end-words of those lines. Notice the repetition, the slightly wavering or rippled reflection of "teas" and "east." Each couplet features this kind of rhyme, as each stanza's final word, in reflection, is respelled from the previous line's endword. We see each thing (tea, fire, a stone) cast back as from water, and altered.

Within the long geographical and historical narrative of *Complaint*, Mann assigns himself a place as well. The book's second strand, in fact, takes the shape of autobiography. As if in partnership with the sensual green environs, many of his finest poems describe an awakening of self, a natural and erotic history of that self. The particular problem or aspect of "complaint in the garden" here derives from Mann's gay narrative, his discovery of sexuality and sexual preference in a place where many dangers lurk—fear, intolerance, eventually the scourge of AIDS. In these poems Mann most fully demonstrates his tonal varieties. "Song" shows his wistful nostalgia for a time "when pornography / was good . . . before the mild age / when all the oversexed / were forced to slip a condom on." He's playful, nearly slain by kitsch, in "Complaint of the Regular," in which his speaker visits a familiar sing-along bar to find a "queen is ruining my favorite song. // Her dress is cherry-red and overlong, / her entrance undercut—it hit a snag." And yet in "Easter, 1996," he cannot suppress the speaker-teacher's awful vision that "AIDS / would not claim just my friends; here and there, AIDS / would take my students, unaware." As the poems proceed, Mann's speaker finds himself, but finds himself often alienated or alone, and so commences another version of that most American narrative to move west-ward, to seek his fortune, or at least his mature life. Still, Florida remains for him, as he asserts with a tinge of irony, both a nostalgic origin and a vision of "the afterlife."

Beyond the two concurrent narratives I've identified, I find a further delightful structural component—that is, Mann's engagement with poetics and poetic history. He is fluent in the generic conventions of the complaint and the pastoral. He is inquisitive and flexible in his fine applications of forms, from sestinas and villanelles to hymnal meter and syllabics. And he is downright gleeful in his echoing of prior poems. I love the witty allusions and spoonerisms, the reflections and reapplications that abound in *Complaint in the Garden*. "About rain, / the weathermen are often wrong," he writes in "Rain," reiterating with a wink Auden's somber entrance in "Musée des Beaux Arts." Yeats makes an appearance, altered, in "this is no country for omens," as does Dylan Thomas in the opening of "The Lady Wishfort," a delightful poem in quantitative syllabics—and in drag: "But when I was young / and glittering below the houselights . . . . " Perhaps I hear a touch of Dickinson in "this is the hour of sprinklers." Mann even relishes punning on the homoerotic possibilities of his own name, as in "Postscriptum": "'You're Randy, Randy Mann,' some guy in shorts / informed me. '*Nice* name.'"

We have before us a skillful, witty, passionate young poet, whose *Complaint in the Garden* represents a rich variety of the American narrative. Randall Mann is both attuned to and at odds with the natural world; he articulates the passions and predicaments of a self inside a massive, arousing, but sometimes brutal culture. And he accomplishes these things with buoyant lyric sensibilities and rejuvenating skills.

—David Baker, series judge and Poetry Editor of *The Kenyon Review*

?

is only something on which to hang
your long overcoat; the slender snake asleep
in the grass; the umbrella by the door;

the black swan guarding the pond.
This ? has trouble in mind: do not ask
why the wind broods, why the light is so unclean.

It is summer, the rhetoric of the field,
its yellow grasses, something unanswerable.
The dead armadillo by the roadside, indecent.

Who cares now to recall that frost once encrusted
the field? The question mark—cousin to the 2,
half of a heart—already has begun its underhanded inquiry.

The Beauty of Things

The world was drowned in dark water:
all was lost. In time, legend says,
from this a new world of weedy greens

was born. But something was missing.
The newly white egrets stared blankly
into the newly white clouds;

the mosquitoes were abuzz with promise:
this was all a long, long time ago.
Then came the men: two men,

the historians have not written, were seen
in the distance, their tanned bodies
covered with dust. And they were alone.

That night, the moon like a lens,
one cooled the other's sunburn
with his tongue. And then they slept.

But they were awakened by rain,
rain inevitable in that overgrown state—
in the absence of the hills, they embraced,

not knowing they were breaking
the seventh rule of love, not knowing
the beauty of things left unrecorded.

Poem Beginning with a Line by John Ashbery

Jealousy. Whispered weather reports.
The lure of the land so strong it prompts
gossip: we chatter like small birds
at the edge of the ocean gray, foaming.

Now sand under sand hides
the buried world, the one in which our fathers failed,
the palm frond a dangerous truth
they once believed, and touched. Bloodied their hands.

They once believed. And, touched, bloodied their hands;
the palm frond, a dangerous truth;
the buried world, the one in which our fathers failed.
Now sand under sand hides

at the edge of the ocean: gray, foaming
gossip. We chatter like small birds,
the lure of the land so strong it prompts
jealousy. Whispered weather reports.

Song

In the grainy yellow artless light
a warmth is in the air.
And our fair hero—shirtless, thin—
flips his feathered hair

and gives someone the eye. What's next
is obvious enough,
suitably raw but loving, almost,
and almost never rough.

Remember when pornography
was good: the body hair,
the actors barely legal? Flicks
from 1984—

past the scary seventies
of bearish men and Crisco,
seeing them fuck to classic rock,
or even worse, to disco—

but still before the mild age
when all the oversexed
were forced to slip a condom on
and get their bottoms waxed.

"There are sites, you know, a few on-line,"
a friend of mine has said,
"that list the names of porno stars,
the ones who end up dead."

These lines are for the age before
the age of styling gel
and muscle queens, for pretty men
with names like Cal and Joel,

whose sort of lethal innocence
is stirring to the soul,
pale and sweet and having *Fun
Down in the Glory Hole.*

Eros

Giving the man behind the counter my money,
I take from him a fresh white towel
and walk into the sex club—the safe
one—called, mythically, Eros.
I go there, as one does, to kill an hour
or two in the hopeful dark.

Out of my clothes, I step into the dark
of the back rooms, where not money
but flesh is the currency of the hour.
I wrap my torso in the towel
and grab a condom: at Eros,
the only sex allowed is safe,

management insisting that we "Play safe
or be thrown out" into the outer dark.
Life's much simpler inside Eros,
where for a little money
I find what I need, in my towel,
cruising the sticky floors for an hour.

But it's been nearly an hour,
and nothing—I am not going to be safe
with just anyone! Then a man without a towel—
beautiful, in the dark—
puts a hand on my chest. He smells like money.
This is why I go to Eros.

(It's hardly my first Eros
experience: there comes an hour
when, in spite of the money,
no matter how unsafe,
I find what I need only in the dark.)
The man without a towel

removes my towel:
I fall into the arms of Eros;
that world, an underworld, dark
no matter the hour.
And it is good. And we are safe.
It is good to have more sex than money.

Complaint of the Regular

The Lady Pearl attempts to sing along—
Thursday's the designated night of drag.
This queen is ruining my favorite song.

Her dress is cherry-red and overlong,
her entrance undercut—it hit a snag.
The Lady Pearl attempts to sing along:

she sashays sluttishly between the throng
of boys and waves a tiny rainbow flag.
This queen is ruining my favorite song:

you see, "A Foggy Day" does not belong
to her: she's white; her wig is carpet shag—
the Lady Pearl attempts to sing along

with Billie Holiday, but all along
her lips are slightly out of synch. This hag,
this queen, is ruining my favorite song.

I come here Thursday nights, and how I long
to look away, but can't. An aging fag,
the Lady Pearl, attempts to sing along.
She cannot help but ruin my favorite song.

Complaint of the Lecturer

The classrooms speak in the language of dust—
when the ancient bell rings, the unattainable

fraternity boys rush to the outside fountain
to absolve themselves. I love to watch them.

Design, industry, and practicality have come together:
the height of the shrubs has been calculated;

the eyes of the plumed mascot are like hard zeros.
In the ladies' toilet are bins for used needles.

Look: on the sidewalk, someone has drawn
a chalk outline of a small dead boy, his white blood;

his hair, perverted into a style much too stylish.
I have learned to hate this emptiness,

the emptying of the dumpsters at dusk,
the emptied offices, the emptied bookshelves,

the empty hands of the head librarian.

Complaint, Poolside

Brushing pollen off my chaise longue,
easing my feet into chlorinated water,
I knew it wasn't paradise. The Florida dust,

thick, oppressive, had yellowed the concrete,
the poplars and scrub oaks been dispossessed,
leaf by yellowed leaf—my life too had fallen

into routine: work, workout, lying out.
Across the water, the chiseled young man
(my old favorite), as always, reading a thick book—

philosophy, maybe? I would have rubbed him
with tanning oil, kissed him hard on the mouth,
but he never returned my not-so-covert stare.

It wasn't paradise. At dusk, when he was gone,
the leathery old men gone, I was the master
of empty chairs. A shock of pink, the sky

went on forever at that hour, the moon
creeping into its corner—paradise, you might say.
If Florida were such a paradise, then why

have I decided to leave? I have forgotten
my reasons, all but one: men go here to die.

Henry James in Jacksonville

Down from charmless Savannah, off the Pullman:
after dinner, he smokes outside his hotel
under the hot-looking stars of Jacksonville—
it matters not a scrap that the public garden,

the prospect, is nearly bare and crude. The Master
sits on a dusky bench and watches the St. John's—
it functions as his Mincio; he's Byron,
fooled by darkness, footlights, velvet air.

There on the dirty little *piazzetta*,
he praises the cheap exoticism, the florid
fountains—but for spiky subtropical things,

he might almost be in a corner of Genoa.
Almost. But Florida's a fearful fraud.
By the palmetto, the pockmarked bellboy, waiting.

The English Angler

Rowland Ward, 1897

We were too early in the season—
no dogwood flowering, just rain
  and violent wind all Sunday—

rattling through dreary Georgian pines.
  The weatherboard homes
sometimes came into view, looking desolate.

  In the middle of the night
we reached Jacksonville; just south,
   one of the swamp bridges was burning—

the repairs kept us six hours waiting.
  To pass the time, the crackers put on white,
played the ghost, scared the blacks into fits . . .

  We were not soon able to understand
the dismal swamps and wilderness haunted
  by torpid alligators; Titian pumas;

the graceful fan-palms, cathedrals
  towering above the forest trees.
The greenery was an English June.

Here the pine trees tapped for turpentine
were dark as flights of buzzards filling the air.
  And the rivers that we crossed.

Palm-lined banks! Reservoirs of water-lilies!
  Visitors from the New England winter
hail the state as their own Riviera, their Italy.

The Heron

A pond the color of Oriental teas.
A heron refusing to look anywhere but east.

Mangroves flecked with a fire,
deep-set birches rife

with the wait for night. In stone,
the heron stares: the stoic tones

of the sky a storied procession of palms;
their red-tipped fronds, overhanging lamps.

Water-bird, it has been centuries since I felt
anything for you. You have been left:

look around. Why does the owl
rest on a goddess's shoulder while you wade so low?

Rain

This is the rain,
the rain in north Florida:
rain on the fanned fronds of the saw palmetto;
on bloodleaf;
on the forked bracts of mock bishop's-weed.

The gray floodgates
of the heavens are open—
thunder, God's rage; random lightning, right as rain.
About rain,
the weathermen are often wrong—

you believe them,
not having yet lost your faith.
Now a storm, soon a cataclysm of rain—
umbrella?
A poncho? No, you have forgotten.

See how water
assaults the lone fireweed,
its ground getting more disturbed. *Never again
will I curse
the ground,* lied God, in the beginning.

The Elements

I *The Mote in the Eye*

The wind instructs the rain: to soak chapeaus
and sprung umbrellas; to flit at light like moths;
to pelt the soil; to swell; to lap at windows—
O punctual monsoons, O sodden months!

The rain instructs the wind: to understand
its gravity; to chip at limestone churchyards;
to sweep its bric-a-brac across the sand,
across the white-patched wings of mockingbirds.

But half the lesson is what isn't taught.
I say the wind will not instruct the rain
in how the sea will hiss and stagger ashore.

O rain, do not instruct the wind that it
is not, in fact, the mouth of the hurricane—
let one betray the other, unaware.

after João Cabral de Melo Neto

II *The Revival of Vernacular Architecture*

Even the habit of the violet hour,
that measured folding-over into dark,
will not compare to rural dusk right there—
no soot, no one on 301. In Starke

the dirt is fine, is civilized—its worth
is undersold, its rows can only mean
that there the earth's unready for rebirth.
And in between the miles of rain, and rain

between a field, and houses sitting dumb,
I saw a tent, undulant; a cross;
the silhouettes of seated souls; a choir.

I stopped the car, I heard some martyrdom
behind the lamplit tarp. Despite wet grass,
I saw a farmer heal his field with fire.

III *The Manmade Lake*

Maples lord over us—the green, the red
ash leaves blur their own mortality.
Lake-side, how easy to forget the dead,
the dark but severed roots of the absentee.

I say we must regret an earlier time:
egrets not yet egrets preening on rock;
wind not a current, not the water's sublime
slap of the rock; the rock not cresting the lake;

the lake not itself . . . the maples, thickset woods;
the only wind the secrets hushed by leaves,
the unrecorded pact between life and death

buried in this place—as if small gods
on Caterpillars, below the forest's eaves,
had not yet parted the waters from the earth.

Angel in Florida

And I, wishing to be back in Cuba,
wandered a room rich with rocking chairs.
Alone on the nightstand,

The Count of Monte Cristo, bound in leather
and dust. Dust the window.
I smudged the panes with my right cuff:

greenhouses of madder crimson Broughtonia;
barbed fences dripping with bougainvillaea;
wildflowers by the roadside, deeper than dye—

but I saw only Broughtonia,
purple cousins of these displaced red ones,
purpling only the mountains of Cuba.

Complaint in the Garden

Sir George Somers, Bermuda, 1609

The slender, leggy spiders
found among our drinking cans
and the linen in the chests—

I blame the month of August.
I blame English seed, the radishes
that came to no proof,

that will never thrive.
I blame a kind of *Melontha*,
the worms I never saw,

the toads, snakes, and creeping,
hurtful beasts I never saw.
I blame archipelagos, all five hundred;

the goodly Bay.
I blame the soil of the entire Island:
one and the same: dark, red,

sandy, dry, and incapable.
My Lord, I blame their god of thunder.

The New World

Cay Bonito, 1804

Ignoring the *Avicennia*, the *Batis*,
the beautiful silver leaves
that held von Humboldt's attention,

his sailors—bored, irritated
at their failure in finding sea crabs—
slowly climbed the mangroves.

And when they found the nests of alcatrases,
young alcatrases, the sailors
hacked them with cutlasses, not out of spite.

And the blackish birds
defended themselves with their pitiful bills.
Not out of spite. And the old ones,

swan-sized, flew above, their calls
hoarse and mournful.
The sea, that cold empire, held no judgment.

The blood that trickled down the trees
did not flower, and the dead,
though winged, did not take flight.

The Shortened History of Florida

The white men far across the unknown ocean.
The one famous dog, named Bercerillo.
The spotted, wrinkled skin of Ponce de León.
The bones littered in Cayo Hueso.

The horses eaten at Apalachicola Bay.
The gold, like lightning: everywhere, nowhere.
The Cradle and the Grave Company.
The water lilies slowly moving toward the shore.

The scars of cannon fire, the fort's reminder.
The French, half-asleep, half-dressed.
The great Turtle Mound near Coronado.

The long-robed friars and the Indian, Peter.
The Indians, who sometimes killed a priest.
The days of lighthouses, before the weather bureau.

Translation of the *Confessionario* into the Local Dialect

Spanish Florida, 1613

I *Father Confessor*

My son, have you cured a man with adulation?
To cure him, did you produce the fire or part
the fire? Have you not searched with the art
of the devil? Have you ever raptured someone?

In order to take the turtle, did you pray?
When the owl sings, have you said, "Do not make noise,"
in hopes that blood would not come out of another's nose?
Have you removed a man from his house today

by singing your charms? Have you said, "Perfuming
the guano with herbs will make him not leave me"?
Have you directed the fish to pray to the sea?
Did you put on the dress skirt when you saw lightning?

If the answers are yes: Son, do not do them again,
and be sorry for them, for they are a sin.

II *The Boy Penitent*

Do I worship the moon and the sun?
I am submissive to the priests. Do I consider
them divine, able to foretell the future?
I will be permitted many wives and children.

Am I much given to thoughts of sodomy?
I know that boys who do it are excluded from men;
are effeminate; are sent to stay with the women;
are placed among hermaphrodites, of whom they say

there are a great many among the Floridians.
But are the true hermaphrodites none other
than these effeminate boys? A hermaphrodite

is not allowed to speak, is put to women's
work. Must carry food and provisions of war.
Is distinguished by its ability to conjure hate.

III *The Church Militant*

My mouth trembling was a sign of something bad.
I did not believe I could be healed with prayers.
I took the liberty to tell past sins to others.
In distress, have I often wished I were dead?

When my eyebrow twitches, it is not a sign of evil.
I have delighted in lewd signals and afterwards
put them into practice. I have said suggestive words.
My desires have been intricate and carnal.

Speaking with an older boy, or embracing,
was I aroused? I have had intercourse with another;
as you say, he investigated me from behind. But did

I consummate the act? I have gone around trying
to do this. I have been both the procurer
and the procuress. I have often wished I were dead.

Je n'ai pas oublié

I have not forgotten the place from which I come.
Not its entryway of dull linoleum;

not the carpet in my room, a spongy green,
my mother's Hoover sucking it clean.

Not those endless afternoons below
the balcony, where I would eat the snow,

selectively, and choose an enemy:
the neighbor's cocker spaniel. Not the boy, me,

saying, *Randy Mann, Randy Mann,*
into the sensual purr of our Carrier fan.

after Baudelaire

The Landscape of Deception

A lone hawk hovers above a corridor
        of gray-boned winter trees
as if it exists only to be admired.
        Early March, the Japanese tulip

in bloom, and the Bradford pear,
        its flowers like boutonnieres—
too white for any boy, any ritual—
        but this is only false spring;

everything here is false, beauty not truth:
        the falling, falling
petals of the Japanese tulip
        already turning ugly,

those petals on the dead grass
        a congregation of deception;
the Bradford pear a lie—
        it will never, to spite its own name,

bear fruit. And the hawk?
        In wait for the small, for the weak,
a lone hawk hovers above a corridor
        of gray-boned winter trees.

Blood

I

My love of blood began when I was ten,
in Lexington—my father sliced his hand
while sawing through some wood. The blood? The blood
was everywhere: it stained the wood, the saw,
the floor of the garage. My father sat
and wrapped his wound; I brought him apple juice.
We never since have spoken of his pain.

II

At twenty-one, I knew there was no cure:
I lusted after men. Legal at last,
I drank the least expensive bottled beer
and blindly followed kindly, foreign men
into their cars, their rented rooms, their beds—
the rest of this is darkness now, is lost.

III

Under the unforgiving bathroom light,
I follow the directions, prick my middle
finger and squeeze until the blood makes red
the white inside the circle. It takes a lot.
Sickened, I lie on the tile and fear results.
The tile is cold. My blood begins to clot.

Old Haunts

I *Smathers Library Men's Room, Second Floor*

What I loved was order:
the four urinals
like boats upended,

tastefully tucked in the corner;
the squares of splotchy
black-on-green linoleum;

the thinning warp of the mirror.
Four foam dispensers,
in the pink—

someone cared.
And lust, on the stalls' actual marble,
no-nonsense, civilized:

"Me: 6'1", 170, slim build,
you: be hairy, clean, healthy,
and not looking to get off."

"No fats, no fems, no trolls.
Bottom seeking top.
Reciprocation is not necessary."

II *Alley Katz Bowling Alley*

Foul air; beer;
locals in stonewashed jeans
leaning against scoring tables

lamplit, ash-stained—
each Thursday, before the bar,
we went bowling.

I took an amateur's pleasure
in the release and long roll
of my borrowed ball,

the pins' fall—when they fell.
It was 1993:
the boys and I

were killing time, we
who couldn't even skip a week
when R. died, then J.

We knew we were not immune.

III *University Club*

Leashed by our friend Amy
dressed head to foot in black—
black heels, black tights,

black her stringy hair,
dyed for the occasion—
Dale and I brought up the rear,

the two of us twins
in cut-off shorts
and combat boots;

in leather jackets,
borrowed; dog collars
from French Addiction

snapped onto our necks;
our thick black eyeliner
the distinguishing mark

of submission,
of the leather slut.
Inside, a wiry man

with a handlebar mustache
stared me down. I was shaken
when I saw my reflection

in the bar mirror,
so I downed Tanqueray
and tonic, hoping to God

none of my students were there.
And when Dale and I were led
onto the dance floor,

when our dominatrix
commanded us to get down
on all fours, when I saw Dale

howl like a wolf
into the houselights,
the bar whooping it up,

I knew. I knew I was in love with him.

Pantoum

If there is a word in the lexicon of love,
it will not declare itself.
The nature of words is to fail
men who fall in love with men.

It will not declare itself,
the perfect word. *Boyfriend* seems ridiculous:
men who fall in love with men
deserve something a bit more formal.

The perfect word? Boyfriend? Ridiculous.
But *partner* is . . . businesslike—
we deserve something a bit less formal,
much more in love with love.

But if partner is businesslike,
then *lover* suggests only sex,
is too much in love with love.
There is life outside of the bedroom,

and lover suggests only sex.
We are left with *roommate*, or *friend*.
There is life, but outside of the bedroom.
My *friend* and I rarely speak of one another.

To my left is my roommate, my friend.
If there is a word in the lexicon of love,
my friend and I rarely speak it of one another.
The nature of words is to fail.

Late Epithalamion

Draped in a rainbow sash, diamond stud
in his right ear, the minister
lit two unity candles, his lover
no help, leering at the two of us instead—

what was the smell? Vanilla? Pear?
Early afternoon in our old apartment,
the wedding there
because the MCC church resembled
a Quonset hut, and I *refused*
to be married in a Quonset hut.

Inside each of us God has placed
the desire to love and to be loved—
the *Requiem*, the wrong Mozart,
blared from the stereo;
dripped wax congealed on the carpet.
When he called for the rings,
I thought of the salesgirl at the mall jewelry store,
awkwardly addressing our hands.
We could afford the cheap white bands.

Will you welcome the newly united couple?
My father then welcomed champagne,
and more champagne . . .

Much later, the plastered minister
would lift his cup in praise of the green
days yet to come.
Outside, the rain like luck
licked our filthy windows clean.

Lament

Given that a palmetto bug
might have been crawling
all over the dirty dishes,

its back wet with the last
of the sink's hard water;
given the small mountain

of laundry, the accusatory colors,
dull whites, indifferent underwear;
given the dust, the heat, the air,

I loved the dark.
On such a night, when sleep came hard,
I was at home and you were all business

at the hospital, under the harsh light,
trying to find the strength
for something like tenderness.

And though I had had enough
of that landlocked town,
of your medical school

that had aged you and made you
bitter; though I was alone,
I offered you this darkness,

in hopes you might return
while it was still dark, love,
while it was still dark.

The Future Tense

Whiter than the roadside rhododendron
I will mistake for hydrangea,
whiter than the whitest lost tourist,

the bread you will fling at the ducks
will lie in fat clumps, the gulls
feasting on the inedible,

their whitish excrement
splattered on our parked car.
There will be immoderate wind:

your hair, for once, will not
be a work of art. This is my fiction.
You will present me with a bottle

of lukewarm white, and even you
will drink right from the bottle—
we'll laugh the way we never laughed.

And you will say the word *love*
as if it were not meaningless, as if
we were not dying, as if our language

were not dying. You will say the word,
love, as if it meant love.

Easter, 1996

There was no vigil: I was up late reading
my students' essays, their polite, meandering words:
Feeling is better portrayed in a film than in its novel;
There's too much analyzing to reading a novel.
I picked up Austen: Elizabeth reading
Darcy's letter, wishing to discredit his words—

but even she couldn't charm me. It was too late.
Had I failed, taught too much too fast,
or had I held something back, straight
from the start? (My students thought I was straight,
I'd seen to that—I knew their prepossessions.) That late
in the millennium, time passed doubly fast:

"next year" was already here, its troubles
too many to write out in verse. Tonight I envisioned
years less like this one, terrible, more complex: AIDS
would not claim just my friends; here and there, AIDS
would take my students, unaware. Their troubles
would be more terrible than I could have envisioned.

Evidence

Blue is the evidence of what I do,
the lies I'll leave behind, no more, no less.
This is the past, and so it must be true.

This stack of DVDs, of overdue
pornography, the titles meaningless:
blue is the evidence of what I do.

This is the coat from Saks Fifth Avenue,
charged to my old American Express—
this is the past, and so it must be true

that once I loved this wretched shade of blue.
I dreamed of men whom I could not impress.
Blue is the evidence of what I do,

the letter here that ends in *I love you.*
My prose was from the heart, my heart a mess.
This is the past, and so it must be true

I lacked the guts to send it off—I knew
of certain things that one should not confess.
Blue is the evidence of what I do.
This is the past, and so it must be true.

Out on the Porch

The afternoon is getting tired,
rocking chairs in an absent-minded wind.

Two tree frogs, green as mint leaves,
sit and stare at nothing in particular.

Beyond the bluegrass, bleached to summer-blond,
the indiscretions of houses boarded up.

Half-painted barns. Plows put out to pasture.
A rural paradise replete with ruins.

South

I

Yellow is the verse,
a cloudless sulphur butterfly.
Yellow are the poplar leaves,
a soldier's dead letters.

Yellow, the recitations:
the sag of sunstruck palmetto fronds
and the bright, new ties of fraternity boys.
The patch of crabgrass poisoned,

the stucco, rain-stained—
yellow the unfounded city of gold.

II

In the wet air, fronds down-turn;
the plated backs of palmetto bugs
glisten like rain.
It is late July, the sky is hot.

Cattle refuse the cattle egrets—
out of their flight I hear heaviness'. . .
You are not the alligator below mangroves;
not the heron,

great blue general,
who slowly lifts his head.
Runaway, you should not be here.
Be somewhere north by now, asleep, asleep.

III

Too many white moths,
their shadows far too large.
And so begins the idling
of yellow buses,

the drivers stepping out to smoke
under a gray sky seceding
from the full moon as it sinks.
This is the hour of sprinklers

on the Southern windows of history
at the darkened Heritage Museum,
of the reflector strips on the heels of the shoes
of the lone runner, of the creep of the pickup truck.

IV

When the last Confederate widow
still sat at home in the damp of shadows,
Confederate jasmine crawling
over a crooked trellis;

when converted men cruised
the streets like crows;
when houses lapsed into the sleep
of history, then so might arise the arsonist,

his South a gray blaze of moonlight,
blue magnolia trees.

Social Life

Hickories. Ash. Feathery-leafed locusts.
The wide green fields lay
in the distance, the cattle

up to their knees in clover, the world
filled with scudding shadows.
Who understood the darkness of the soil

under the broad lapping leaves
of mottled tobacco?
Robins foraging in the grass

for their greedy yellowthroated chicks;
or far off, in the dirt, white-shirted,
singing ploughers following their slow

teams in the fresh furrows?
On the long porch of the weatherboard home,
the young gentlemen veiled

their evil, their doctrine—
maxima reverentia pueris debetur—
that of a language long dead.

Elegy for the Hurdler

1971-1989

The track was hot, the lanes were hard and black—
    remember? You didn't even want to run.
Anthony Solomon, if you came back,
    back to the day when we were almost men,

then wouldn't others on the team return,
    somehow, to find a way to keep you off
the track that afternoon, to make you turn,
    turn back? Return—the school will look as if

you hadn't left. Forget the ambulance;
    the asphalt, bloody, burned—you never died.
Come back. Your starting block forbids your stance.
    Your hurdles lowered, stacked, and set aside.

Yard Sale

The early birds arrive before the sun;
they park their cars up on the neighbors' grass.
We sell Grandmother's things off, one by one.

Even before my father and I are done
labeling her furniture, *en masse*
the early birds arrive, before the sun.

Her dishes are among the first things gone—
Corelle, that setting of the middle class.
We sell Grandmother's things off, one by one:

knitting needles, buttons, yarn, a ton
of safety pins. The things that they amass,
those early birds, arrived before the sun.

By eight o'clock the yard is overrun.
We move her clothes, her single demitasse;
we sell Grandmother's things off, one by one . . .

Father, it's late. Remove the signs. First son,
forget the unsold still-lifes on her grass.
Forget that early birds arrived before the sun
to cart your mother's things off, one by one.

Fiduciary

the relationship between
    blackbird and fence post, between
the cow and its egret, the field
    and wildflowers overrunning the field—
so little depends upon their trust.

    Here, in God we trust
to keep our cash and thoughts in line—
    in the sky, an unexplained white line
could be the first of many omens.
    But this is no country for omens,

the line as chalky as the moon,
    bleak and useless as the moon
now rising like a breath of cold air . . .
    There is gullibility in the air.

The Lady Wishfort

But when I was young
and glittering below the houselights
    in my beaded taffeta
        and tiara,
        and honored by all

    but the leather boys
as the Princess of the Wedding Gowns,
    and every Saturday night
        blushing on cue—
        Ave Maria

    was my name back then.
And the queens of greater Orlando
    came out in force to see me
        pretend to wed
        some lucky straight boy

    chosen from the crowd.
Each Saturday I wore a new gown.
"Love Will Keep Us Together,"
        "We've Only Just
        Begun"—I did *all*

    the seventies songs
worth a damn. But too soon Orlando
    switched to disco Inferno,
        lovesick lip-synch
        my six-month downfall.

It's been twenty years
since I packed up my duct tape. I'm back.
Now? I wear a girdle. Now
    I paint my face
    with a thicker base.

Postscriptum

At first I was confused: the afterlife
looked like Florida, the fiery sand;
the company of tan, half-naked men;
the wayward, wilting palms. South Beach, I thought.

"You're Randy, Randy Mann," some guy in shorts
informed me. "*Nice* name." I was at a loss.
"You're new. See the queen who's eyeing you?
That's Brunetto." I saw Latini, bronzed;

I smelled the brimstone—then I understood . . .
During the day, I'm damned to perfect my tan.
When prone, I often write the truth in sand:
Dante lied. My fellow sodomites

and I do not regret a blessèd thing:
we loved the only way we knew. That's that.
We choose to walk, not for fear of being cursed
a century—we mingle. Socialize.

There is no rain, or rain of fire, or fire—
actually, the Seventh Circle's rather nice,
and all my friends are here. The truth? It's buried
somewhere beneath the surface—there lies Dante,

over on the sand, wearing a thong.

The End of the Last Summer

The good white laundry
        dreamlike between white dogwoods;
the Spanish moss; the palm-flanked
        Baptist churches
along the small hill of Eighth Avenue—

        none of this matters.
            This landscape is just too much.
The termites are too busy,
        eating the heart
of the wood of the houses of the dead.

        —Seven years have passed
        since the red, long-faced tourists
mailed their glossy postcards home,
        regaling friends
with tales of the Gainesville student murders.

        All is as it was
        before the murders. The dead?
Names spray-painted on a wall;
        trees providing
shade for the brick, the undergraduates.

        It's time to leave now.
        The old professors have gone
on sabbatical, across
        the Atlantic
to visit their favorite fallen empires.

The hidden tree frogs
        have begun to chirp again.
The peninsula grows dark;
        the dead stay dead.
The sea is rising . . . and the world is sand.

NOTES

"Henry James in Jacksonville": James's *The American Scene* (1907), chapter fourteen, is the source of the details of the poem.

"The English Angler": The poem uses details and phrases from Rowland Ward's *The English Angler in Florida* (1898).

"Angel in Florida": This poem is for Angel Cuadra.

"Complaint in the Garden": Many of the details are taken from William Strachey's *True Reportory of the Wracke* (1610). He and Sir George Somers were shipwrecked on Bermuda in 1609. Somers squared out a garden on the island but failed to grow any food.

"The New World": The source drawn upon is Alexander von Humboldt's *The Island of Cuba* (1856).

"The Shortened History of Florida": This poem is for Jamie McKendrick.

"Translation of the *Confessionario* into the Local Dialect": Several of the phrases are adapted from Francisco Pareja's *Confessionario* (1613).

"Social Life": The poem takes some phrases from Thomas Nelson Page's *Social Life in Old Virginia* (1892).

"The End of the Last Summer": The last line is taken from Wilfred Owen's "To—."